CONSEQUENCES OF CHOICE

DECISIONS THAT DEFINE US

Lokendra Singh

INDIA • SINGAPORE • MALAYSIA

ISBN 979-8-89133-892-0

To my dearest Suchita, Aadya,
and my guiding stars, my parents,

In the pages of 'Consequences of Choice,' I aim to capture not just the decisions that shape our lives but the profound impact of your love and wisdom. Suchita, your unwavering support is the bedrock of my journey, and in Aadya, I find a living testament to the beautiful consequences that love unfurls.

To my parents, your guidance forms the silent but powerful undercurrent, shaping the choices I make. This book is a tribute to the intertwined tapestry of our family, where each choice echoes with the resonance of our shared love.

With heartfelt gratitude and love,
Lokendra Singh

Review by

Mr. K. C Mani – Chairman & Managing Director,
BDB India Private Limited

An excellent book that will be useful for students, young professionals who are on the path to building their careers, and professionals who are keen to build leadership positions and reach the top at a young age.

The author beautifully narrated how "Shiva, the main character in this book overcame the challenges and struggles during studies, finding a job, building the career and all the experiences helped him to travel smoothly across and through the corporate ladder and reach the top at a younger age. It also explained the traits behind the decision-making process at various stages of the personal and professional field. The most interesting part of this book is, that it is replete with adequate examples of areas that influence decision-making on personal and professional fronts.

The book dwells on the dynamics followed by different levels of professionals in the corporate world and the impact of empathy towards young professionals by top management for making the right decisions and how it helps in building the career. The author demonstrated this quality of "empathy" by top management through excellent examples. The book articulates a series of corporate events and the "right attitude" that helps to build a career by developing a team and the importance of team building for self and organizational development.

The author demonstrated the work-life balance and choices made through conscious or unconscious routes through examples. The magic of qualities like patience, persistence, and PR is very well narrated, and it works wonderfully for building a rewarding career.

A must-read book for students, young professionals, and professionals aiming to reach the top at an early age.

Contents

Foreword

LOOKING BACK, I do not remember my first meeting with Lokendra, but it was a combination of destiny and choice. About twelve years ago, I was in Chennai with no plan to move to Pune. But fate brought an opportunity, and I moved to Pune. After some years, the love to meet and hear Indian business leaders at a book club reading about their experiences brought us together.

Other business forums continued the frequent meetings. Casual acquaintance, over a period of time, became friendship. Until then, friends had developed only during early life, in schools and colleges, but rarely in a job. Destiny brought us together, but our choices have sustained the friendship.

Lokendra has amazed me with his capacity to take steps to move up continuously. He learns by reading books and through lending programmes, but does not keep it to himself. He shares his knowledge with others. Lokendra is not a typical workaholic leader, but enjoys life, travelling and other forms of fine art—such as music and poetry. Lokendra uses his mind, heart and gut.

He can follow a plan, yet break free to change course if his heart tells him so. Lokendra has a spiritual side that builds a distance from the material world, yet enjoys the finer things of life. He is a creator wanting to do something 'perfect', or 'ideal', in real life. He is yet balanced by practical wisdom to make things happen.

Lokendra is a 'Yogi' and a 'Raja' at the same time—a thinker and a business leader. So, he has amazed me again by becoming an author although, looking back, I should not have been surprised.

This book differs from others in the same genre of other books inspiring leadership that has been written. Many books by authors or biographers are of people who have suffered severe setbacks and, with herculean effort, become superheroes. Some books are about great business leaders who founded and led large corporations.

Although readers are awed by the lives of such people, most do not relate to such leaders. Readers get a feeling of inadequacy. But Shiva of this book is someone most people can relate to. Shiva is a typical, lower middle-class person brought up with limited means and one who wants to break out of mediocrity. The instances of Shiva's life are easy to understand and follow in ours.

Shiva reflects the life and philosophy of Lokendra. We may be born in given circumstances, but the choices and risks we take can help us break out of them. At every stage, we can do something more with our life. I highly recommend this book to everyone who wants to understand how ordinary folks can make daily choices to improve their lives and shape their destiny.

I look forward to Lokendra authoring many more books and sharing his thoughts, observations and experiences.

Pushpendra Singh
Executive Coach,
Ex – MD, Leoni Cables

Preface

Dear Readers,

It is with great pleasure and a sense of profound fulfilment that I present to you this book, the culmination of endless days—and nights—of contemplation. And passion!

This book reflects my deep curiosity about life and how Choices define Life in its totality. Some choices lead you to the top and some drag you down. But, finally, it is a choice made by an individual. I have used small stories and anecdotes of Shiva's life to explore how his choices defined his life's journey.

As an author, my purpose is not to provide definitive answers to doubts and queries that cast their shadows on the lives of all of us; neither to claim absolute knowledge. Instead, I aspire to ignite the flame of curiosity within you, to inspire contemplation and to encourage you to embark on your own voyage of self-discovery.

It is my fervent hope that this book will serve as a catalyst for conversation, a source of inspiration and a companion on your individual quest for meaning. May its words resonate with you, provoke new perspectives and spark profound conversations that transcend the boundaries of these pages.

I extend my deepest gratitude to those who have supported me throughout this endeavour. To my loved ones—my wife Suchita, daughter Aadya and my parents, whose unwavering belief in my abilities sustained me through the darkest of times.

A special thanks to Angshuman Bonnerjee—Senior Editor and News Editor of several leading newspapers and journals across the country—for guiding me through the writing process and helping me structure my thoughts, edit and format the book for an outcome as beautiful as *Consequences of Choice*.

Thanks also to all my mentors and teachers who have shared their wisdom for my professional—and personal—growth and nurtured me to spread my wings in this wide world.

And, above all, thanks to you, Dear Reader, for embarking on this journey alongside me. With every turn of a page, may you find a renewed sense of wonder, a newfound appreciation for the intricacies of existence and the courage to embark on your own, unique path.

Embrace that journey, for it is within that journey that we find our true selves.

Sincerely,

Lokendra Singh

Chapter I

Work-Life Balance?

What Is All the Rigmarole About?

Do we keep our life aside when we work?
Or, do we keep our work aside
when we live?

HE WAS DEAD. Stone cold dead! But then, Amit Grewal, 28, had died many times before this early dawn of October 6, 2020...

The last few times were when he felt mortified after being admonished by his boss at his workplace—a high-end software services department of the company—for not being up to scratch and be able to meet the high standards set by the company. But only he knew, and his God knew, that he had tried really hard to strike a balance between his exacting 8:00-23:00 hours work schedule and the measly 2-3 hours' time that he had left to himself after accounting for his physical needs.

This time, however, there was the irrefutable testimony of a suicide note left not far from the sightless, lifeless body that hung limply from the end of a rope tied to the hanger clamps of the three-bladed fan that broke the unmitigated paleness of the whitewashed ceiling. He must have been dangling like that for hours, his face a mixture of blue and mottled grey, before they found him...

The note, itself, was not much verbose, only about four or five lines where Amit had absolved any person, known or unknown, of any wrongdoing, or causing him bodily, or mental, harm. What struck one more was the fact that he had, in fact, held himself—and his own inability to adjust to his very demanding work schedule—responsible for taking this extreme step.

His personal life, he stated plainly in the note, had been suffering immensely from a lack of 'work-life balance' and had 'wreaked havoc on his relationships' in and outside of his job, even seriously jeopardizing the only amorous relationship he had in life—that with 24-year-old Smita.

But what Amit had overlooked—even forgotten—under the pressures of everyday living was that work had been the very basis of his life, his dreams and aspirations—in fact his very existence—ever since the time he had donned his graduation cap and cape and walked out of university!

SHIVA SAT IN HIS OFFICE CHAMBER, a huge sheaf of papers—many of them marked 'Important', 'Immediate Attention', 'Urgent', or 'For Your Information', although not necessarily in that order—was piled up in front of him. His spectacle frame was drawn up from his eyes so that they were now hiding his forehead, but not enough to mask the deep furrows and ridges that marked it. Somewhere at the edge of the large, mahogany wood desk, his mid-morning cup of coffee was going cold, untouched. The Amit Grewal incident—as the whole office was by now gossiping about it—had shaken him more than he would care to admit in public.

It may sound blunt, very blunt indeed, reflected Shiva—some people called him Sambhu—and may even hurt the sentiments of the teeming multitude of career-seekers who are also on an eternal quest to strike a 'work-life balance', but it is only foolish and misguided youngsters like Amit who seek to separate their *work avatar* from their *life avatar*!

They fail to appreciate that 'work' and 'life' are two sides of the same coin, and one cannot be sifted out from the other without rendering the residue useless.

'Work', as Shiva well knew, for everyone starts as an avenue for generating enough money to sustain oneself and one's family—just as it had done for Amit. A young person who has just graduated from college starts looking for a way to earn his or her livelihood. And the basis for finding the means to earn this livelihood is one's educational qualifications, based on which any employer hires the services of novices and trainees. In the beginning, the joy and excitement of landing one's first job transcend all other emotions.

The new recruits are groomed within the organization to become relevant to the requirements of their chosen field. And there begins the irony! Once a person starts gaining a certain amount of experience and the salary goes northwards, expectations from one's job (read work) and life, too, tend to grow exponentially. Soon, marriage follows. But what *is* a happy marriage without buying a roof over one's head?

What *is* a genteel way of commuting to the workplace other than in one's own car?

These aspirations, in their own right, have a place in everyone's life, mused Shiva, and there is nothing wrong with them as such! But he well understood that, through all these life's ventures, there should be no cause for complaining—especially about the very 'work' that provides these basic amenities of 'life'.

Having started out on one's career on a jubilant note after landing that plum job following graduation which laid the foundation for all later aspirations, there should be no cause to blame the same job even as liabilities—although salary not so much—increase to a great extent. Or, indeed, blame one's failure to adjust to new and changed responsibilities as a mismatch in one's 'work-life balance'!

***

SHIVA HAD ONCE EMPLOYED an ambitious, hardworking woman—31-year-old Malini—who had been away from her husband for several years after marriage. So, she wanted to leave her current job and shift to the town where he worked—where, in fact, Shiva's company was located. Being able to stay with her husband was the trigger for her decision.

"Sir, I'd be very glad if you could give me a chance to work for your company," she said.

"Why do you want to leave your current job?" Shiva asked her the next inevitable question any interviewer asks a potential candidate.

"Sir, I've been away from my husband for over three years now. He works in a manufacturing firm here. I'd like to relocate to this city from where I live because *I want to stay with him*," she was quite emphatic about the last part of that sentence. Did he hear a faint note of pleading in her voice? Shiva wondered.

Anyway, Shiva's company—it was in the business of manufacturing mixer-blenders and drying equipment for a wide range of process industries—put her through the regular grind of tests that they usually asked all newcomers to take and found that she was the right fit they were looking for. So, they shook hands and she, on her part, got the town of her choice. Things went smoothly for a month or so.

Then, one fine morning, she traipsed up to Shiva's office room, knocked on the door and waited till he asked her to enter.

“Yes, what is it Malini?” Shiva looked inquiringly at her lifting his head from the papers lying on the table in front of him and squinting up at her through the top of his rimless spectacles.

“It’s about my commute to office, Sir,” she spoke a little haltingly.

“Yes, what of it?”

“Well Sir, you know, I live pretty far off from office, almost at the other end of town,” she said. “So, I have to take a lot of trouble, and time—over an hour, at least—to reach office in time every day. And, recently, I’ve even started getting late on quite a few occasions.”

Well, well, thought Shiva. Here it comes! She had already started complaining—although low key, at first, as usually happens in such cases.

“May I have a pick-up and drop by the office, Sir?” she continued.

But the company was not in a position to do that since it would entail huge logistical issues given the number of eligible employees that it had like Malini.

Shiva reasoned with her that she had known everything before she accepted the job offer and joined the company. He well understood, of course, that her priority at that time was moving from one city to another where her husband lived. But she had—even before a month or so had passed—conveniently forgotten what her *basic priority* had been, based upon which she had taken her decision of her own free will. She had now found fresh grounds for complaining about her workplace!

This is usually the way things happen in a person's life, as it did with Amit's. Having sown the seeds of conflict and, so, confrontation with the organization, newer areas of grievances crop up slowly. And allusions like, 'We aren't considered for the pains we take for coming to office despite the many difficulties in our lives,' turn disagreement and displeasure into pure frustration with one's 'work-life balance'. And so, the cup of despondency runs over, first giving way to despair, and then to desperation, leading to morbid endings as happened in Amit's case!

What both Malini and Amit had conveniently forgotten, reflected Shiva, was that it is 'work' which keeps motivating us to forge further ahead in 'life' fulfilling our basic needs and desires. And 'life' continues to flourish the more we 'work', since it is 'work' which allows us to interact, develop, create and showcase our abilities to do better, in the process helping us to satiate all our material needs and indulge in the small pleasures of life, like going out for a candle-lit dinner, taking a pleasure trip abroad, or even a cruise on a luxury liner if we are fortunate.

Without the yoke of 'work' round our necks, these necessities—and, yes, luxuries—would remain unfulfilled, mused Shiva. It is only 'work' that helps us earn a living, allowing us to put food on our and our loved ones' plates, pay for their education, our travel and so on.

A job that started with generating income slowly starts losing its initial charm as we begin to add liabilities to our life which often exceed our income. We are slowly sucked into a quagmire of EMIs for a car or a house, or credit cards for activities to show off to the world, hitting us badly where it hurts—our devotion to our 'work'! 'Life' would lose all meaning without the ability to earn a living through 'work'.

***

THERE IS NO DEARTH of employee-dominated social media platforms that are 'self-expression' areas where people write whatever they wish to, whenever they wish to which they might never have got the chance to do earlier. One of the recent posts Shiva had seen was about: 'What HR Gives versus What Employees Want'. If one looks at this 'debate' closely, whatever HR gives are the 'static needs' which a person has; it is assumed that these 'needs' should anyway be taken care of. When we undergo a training programme, Shiva ruminated, our 'static need' for that programme is to take training, understand the concepts and emerge out of it with some knowledge of the subject and its implementation in our day-to-day work.

Training provided by organizations is meant to ensure that employees are kept updated with the current technology or behavioral aspects. This is the 'basic, or 'static', need of any employee who undergoes a training programme. And both trainer and trainee are well aware of this. The trainee is a first-timer and all his or her 'basic' needs are met. He, or she, has never undergone any training earlier. So, the trainee's basic aim would be to imbibe the knowledge imparted by the trainer. Now, suppose, thought Shiva, what could happen if the trainer liked the class and was pleased with the outcome? So, beyond the scope of fulfilling the 'basic' or 'static' needs of his trainees, he gives away a few things which were not part of the programme but were 'implied' throughout its duration. And, he may well offer a gift to each of the trainees at the end of the course!

Then, when the same set of people attends some other training programme, the gift the trainer gave away with such largesse becomes their 'static' need, although it was 'implied' in the first instance. Thus, an 'implied' need now becomes a 'static' need. Shiva had more than a vague suspicion that this was what was happening with the young generation nowadays.

Some things which were never a part of 'giveaways' by organizations even a few years ago have slowly been converted from 'implied' needs to 'static' ones. Even an employer showing appreciation for work well done is considered a 'basic', or 'static', need by the employee. Denial of this need at any level becomes a reason for disquiet among many in the workforce, especially among the younger generation, as they have not seen many failures in life as their parents would have seen.

Whatever is provided by any organization or institute is for the well-being of its employee, who believes he, or she, is inherently deserving of these privileges and so takes them for granted.

***

So, SPEAKING OF 'work-life balance', do we keep our 'life' aside when we 'work'? Or, do we keep our 'work' aside when we 'live'? This is the question one must ask oneself first. Shiva, deep down in his heart, wanted to be an instrument of change and guide such confused people as Amit or Malini by trying to see how they could reflect on 'life' and 'work' through the same prism in a way which made them happy and contented.

This philosophy had been etched into Shiva's mind for the past 22 years and he tried to implement this at all the stages of his life—whether on the personal or the work front.

Chapter II
Choice versus Destiny

What Not to Do

Is 'destiny' something that was written before we were born? Or is it something we write because of the conscious 'choices' we make throughout our lives?

LIFE, BY DEFINITION, should be fairly simple—'B-C-D'. Or, at least, Shiva thought so! It starts with Birth (B) and ends with Death (D). Choice (C) is what one is faced with on one's journey between points B and D, which makes it what it is today. We do not have any control over the family or the circumstances—rich or poor—in which we are born; but we do have control over the innumerable *choices* that we make on that journey between B and D.

Whenever things go especially wrong, we tend to say, "This is my destiny!" But is it really our 'destiny', or the result of all the choices we have made until that point of time? Shiva always wondered what the real meaning of 'destiny' is. Is it something that was written *before* we were born? Or is it something we, ourselves, created because of the *conscious choices* we made throughout our lives?

When we search a little deeper, we understand that 'destiny' has nothing to do with someone else writing your fate, but you yourself. The world may thrust upon us some situation we may or may not have any control over, but what we do or make with that situation determines our destiny.

From the day we are born, we are faced with contradictory claims that our lives are predestined and that Fate deals us the cards we have to play at the game of Three Card Poker, or that our life is the result of our choices, shaping it all the way from the cradle to the grave.

Shiva still remembered the lyrics of the haunting and melodious folk-song, *The Gambler*, written by the relatively obscure Don Schlitz, and turned into a No. 1 hit on Billboard's country music chart by Kenny Rogers in 1978. Schlitz's story of a late-night card game on a train that was apparently 'bound for nowhere' might be the greatest Rogers song of all time:

On a warm summer's evenin'/ On a train bound for nowhere/ I met up with a gambler/ We were both too tired to sleep,/ So we took turns at starin'/ Out the window at the darkness,/ Till boredom overtook us/ And he commenced to speak...

He said, "Son, I've made a life/ Out of readin' people's faces/ And knowin' what their cards were/ By the way they held their eyes. So, if you don't mind me sayin'/ I can see you're out of aces,/ For a taste of your whiskey,/ I'll give you some advice..."

So, I handed him my bottle/ And he drank down my last swallow/ And then, he bummed a cigarette,/ And then he bummed a light.../ And the night got deathly quiet/ His face lost all expression/ He said, "If you're gonna play the game, boy,/ You gotta learn to play it right...

"'Cause every gambler knows/ That the secret to survivin'/ Is knowin' what to throw away/ And knowin' what to keep,/ 'Cause every hand's a winner/ Just like every hand's a loser/ And the best that you can hope for/ Is to die in your sleep...

"You gotta to know when to hold up,/ Know when to fold up,/ Know when to walk away, Know when to run.../ And you never count your money/ When

you're sittin' at the table/ There'll be time enough for counting/ When the dealin' is done."

And when he finished speakin',/ He turned back toward the window,/ He crushed out his cigarette/ And faded off to sleep/ And somewhere in the darkness,/ The gambler he broke even,/ But in his final words,/ I found an ace that I could keep...

"You gotta know..."

***

SHIVA'S FATHER HAD started his job as a stenographer in the Indian Railways. He had lost his father as a child and his elder brother took care of the family. Shiva's dad had had to carry on with his studies while he was working. Being from a not-so-well-off family and trying to meet the basic needs, he had also worked as a typist in his teen years at the Krishna Temple at Janambhoomi, in Mathura. The establishment was then held by the Birlas. The family had never had anyone with a professional degree, such as Engineering.

Even though Shiva's Dad rose to quite a high level professionally speaking, salaries in government jobs in those days did not allow one to provide a good education to one's children, especially if there were three mouths to feed. He had chalked out his own career path by educating himself and sitting for various internal examinations in the Railways and Shiva half suspected that his father wanted him to follow in his footsteps, as most parents tend to do.

So, Shiva's father kept prodding him to take all the Railway Recruitment Board (RRB) examinations, which Shiva secretly never even wanted to pass. He knew that, if he got through, his entire life would revolve round the Railways just as his father's had. He had seen his father struggle and knew how difficult it was to rise in a government job from a lowly start. Shiva, for one, had taken an early decision never to be a part of it!

The struggles in one's life show one the correct path to take and provide a good insight into what one *should not* be doing. Determined to go beyond a 9 to 5 government job, Shiva had already made up his mind to join the booming private sector.

After passing his Class XII Board examinations and not knowing what to do next, Shiva applied almost anywhere he could. Being a Science student opened up endless studying opportunities for him—Bachelor of Science, Bachelor of

Engineering, Bachelor of Medicine and Bachelor of Surgery (MBBS), or even Bachelor of Dental Surgery (BDS).

At that time, Tata Motors was recruiting high school graduates as apprentices, training them and utilizing the skills they gained at the shop-floor level. One of Shiva's friends advised him to appear for the examination and the subsequent interview, which Shiva unhappily did, since he did not want to take up the job.

"I don't want to take up that job, Dad! I want to study further and not work...I think I'm too young for it," Shiva confided in his father.

"But I'd like you to get into a job as I did after passing my Class VII exam, son."

As the job had come through Shiva's father, he knew he had to oblige him. But, soon afterwards, he was in a dilemma as he was lucky enough to have secured admission simultaneously to an engineering course and a call for a Tata Motors job on the same date in 1996—a date he still could not forget! His dad was excited, too, that his son had the option to choose a job over an engineering course. The latter was very expensive, while a job had the potential to earn money at that young age, although it was, in hindsight, quite a short-term vision.

Shiva and his father weighed all the pro-s and con-s and held some intense discussions and parleys.

"I'd like to go for the engineering course, Dad, and give up that Tata Motors job offer. I'm not ready for employment and I have much more to do in life," Shiva protested.

Shiva's father looked him in the eye. Shiva stared back, defiant. Unflinching! His father was the one to lower his gaze. Somehow, he knew he had to relent and send Shiva to an engineering college despite the prohibitive expenses. Even much later in life, Shiva would remember all the sacrifices his father had to make by taking up that enormous financial burden while his siblings were still in school.

But Shiva was happy! He had won the first round with 'destiny', said 'No' to his father's wish. He had made his own 'choice', which was to shape his career later in life.

***

THE DECISIONS ONE TAKES do not necessarily determine the course of one's life over the next two or three years, but, sometimes, even a decade or two later! Not the least of all decisions is that of what *not* to do!

Shiva's roommate, Manish, was struck by jaundice and fell very ill in the very first year of their engineering course. They were both not from financially sound families and neither his friend nor Shiva—although *that* question did not arise here—could have managed to get admitted to a hospital in a strange city miles away from their hometown. Their college was in a remote location far from the city and they stayed in a boarding on the campus. Worse still, it was exam time!

But Shiva did not think twice before he took his decision. Manish was his friend and he was in need of help... any kind of help! And Shiva would not be the one to demur, or deny him that help if he could. He decided to skip his exams, picked Manish literally out of his sickbed and carried him straight to the bus terminus where they boarded the long-distance bus to Manish's house in another town around five hours away from their college. Manish sitting for any of his exams was clearly out of the question!

Manish was smart and, although he was absent for all the subject tests in that first semester, he cleared them all in the second along with his subjects in the current semester. Shiva felt proud of Manish and also satisfied deep down inside that he had been the one to take him home. If Manish had missed a whole year in college, Shiva knew he would not be able to forgive himself. He was pleased that *he* was the only one among their friends who had been courageous enough to have taken that decision, even at the cost of dropping out of one subject exam himself.

Shiva had said '*no*' to his own keen desire to take the exam—he had, indeed, been well-prepared for it!—his burning ambition to bask in the self-aggrandizement of scoring high marks far above what his peers would be credited with. There are certain moments in life when *you cannot measure satisfaction like pouring out a spoonful of sugar into a coffee cup*, thought Shiva.

***

ONE INCIDENT HAS LEFT AN INDELIBLE MARK on Shiva's mind. During the last year of his engineering course, he and his friends were staying in a bachelors' pad (the word originated in Beatnik speech in 1959 and later found place in Hippie slang; in its original English sense, it meant a 'temporary place to sleep in'). It was an independent house right in the heart of Kolhapur city in Maharashtra. The house belonged to a District Judge who was employed in Ahmednagar in the same state.

He rented out his house to students like Shiva, throwing in a bed-and-breakfast offer along with dinner, although not on weekends. And never lunch. Weekend fast-food binges and weekday lunches were meant to be eaten away from their mess room canteen. The canteen constituted a sprawling mattress on the floor, a washbasin for after-meal cleaning up, two cats in the yard outside which often made their stealthy way to their plates and bowls if left unattended for a moment, and a ceiling fan that whirred noisily overhead in unison with the speed of the regulator as it had not been oiled in many months.

For the weekday lunches—better call it midday snacks!—Shiva and his friends had to scour the eateries in the areas around where they happened to be on a particular day. They were four people staying in a two-room lodging with a kitchen, while the other half of the tenement building was permanently locked up with discarded and unused items of the house dumped in small rooms where mice and lizards had a free run of the place.

One weekend, the landlord dropped in on them while on a visit to the town to check on the house. They placed a chair in the open space in front of the house—a garden patch overrun with weeds and shrubs trapped in morass and cobwebs. A few house geckos chuck-chuck-chucked in the shadows. As Shiva and company spent most of their time there studying, they rarely managed to 'maintain the garden'. They sat on the small steps leading to the house with the District Judge sitting in the rickety chair they had pulled up for him.

Shiva thought to himself half-grinning at his own witticism that, whenever and wherever a judge decided to pull up a chair, he could hold court. *That* became his court. But not this time! The District Judge was simply being friendly and delving into their young minds to fathom what they really wanted from the life that they were leading...what rich colours of prints of their checkered lifestyle instantly upped the 'boho chic quotient' of their everyday existence.

Shiva was the most outspoken and talkative of the group and the onus fell on him mostly to carry on with the Judge a conversation on various topics. They, finally, settled on two aspects of his life's journey—*how he had become a judge* and *what he was looking for in life*. He must have been in his 50s as far as the youngsters could guess. He spoke at length on how he wanted to become a High Court judge and what his plans for doing this were.

In retrospect, maybe the seeds of Shiva's plans for his own future and career were sown by this Judge. Here was a man well past his prime, who was already a District Judge, and he was still charting out his forward moves, while his group of friends—in their early stages of completing graduation—had never even given a thought to what they would like to do next, which industry they would like to join, or in which field they would like to work in an industry of their choice...!

Engineering graduates are often all at sea in figuring out how an industry works in real-time. And, during those days, classroom syllabuses laid more stress on the technical, or theoretical—rather than the practical—aspects of any branch of engineering. So, all four of them who were barely crossing over from day to a seemingly endless day without aspirations—or, at least, the faintest of ideas of how to make their aspirations come true—had found an elderly person igniting a rocket of ambition beneath them while speaking of his own career progression.

It lit more than an inquiring spark in Shiva's mind about what he needed to do in future as soon as he had sat for his final examinations. Shiva still did not rule out the possibility of this being one of the reasons that he was employed well before the final results came out and he walked out in his graduation cape and cap with an engineer's degree!

***

When Shiva had completed his engineering course, he moved out for training at a steel plant. But he soon found out that he was not cut out for a shift worker's job. Sales and marketing was what he always thought was meant for him and this inspiration took firm roots in his mind when he found that the steel plant had a Vice-President, Commercial, who was in his mid-30s.

Looking around, Shiva found that he had supervisors who had completed almost half of their career. It had been quite a difficult task for them to reach there, which he could realize even at that young age. The instance of the Vice-President,

Commercial, had fired his imagination and he decided one day during his training program that he would become a Marketing Director at the age of 30. Shiva's sights were set much higher despite the fact that he was aged 22 at the time!

***

SHIVA WAS LUCKY ENOUGH to find an able guide and mentor at the very beginning of his career. He was the most talkative youngster among the crop of new recruits in the company and tried to do things a little differently than the others during his training program, which his manager appreciated and encouraged. He tried his best to implement whatever he had learnt during his engineering course.

The most significant lesson that Shiva tried to weave into his daily job was the 'time study' he did for his manager to increase productivity. The details of that are inconsequential here, but the manager seemed impressed and took a liking to him. Shiva, sometimes, used to speak of introducing different facets into the work schedule which might not always have been feasible for his manager to implement, but he may have found something in Shiva that he liked.

One fine morning, Shiva's manager called him to his room and told him, "You should move on to sales and marketing—the plant is not for you. Don't waste your time here."

Shiva had, however, already decided on this course and kept nudging one of his friends, a year senior to him, who was in sales to find a job for Shiva in his company whenever a job opportunity in sales and marketing would present itself. So, in due course, Shiva's friend informed him of an opening as a Marketing Engineer. Shiva jumped at the offer, left his training at the steel plant and moved to the new job as a starry-eyed Marketing Engineer.

He still believed that, when you know your goal at an early stage of life, it helps a lot!

***

AFTER JOINING THE small-scale company almost straight out of college with zero experience of sales, Shiva didn't realize that he had entered a world where jobs would be scarce and joblessness of colossal proportions. Had he stayed on with his training at the steel plant, he would have been absorbed there after a brief while and would have earned enough to sustain himself, if not a family.

He would have had a place to stay, food on his plate and money to spend at least on the bare necessities.

But the new job hit Shiva hard where it hurt most! Not only were salaries never paid in full, but he also had to arrange for his own lodging, and even food became difficult to come by. He used to live in a bachelors' apartment with the rest of his college mates. Shiva's closest friend and he were the only ones who were close to calling themselves 'employed' compared to the others whom they took care of in spite of not getting paid for months on end. Shiva, in those days, cam very close to knowing what 'living from hand to mouth' really meant!

Even when they *did* get paid, the money came in dribs and drabs—small amounts, really, as daily-wage workers get, and spread out over long periods of time. Shiva's employer would actually draw out a wad of notes from his pocket in front of them and—licking his forefinger to make it wet enough to be able to count the notes without an extra one or two slipping through—give them, maybe, five hundred-rupee notes to make it really look like he was handing out a full five hundred. Somewhere, Shiva felt the man derived a vicarious pleasure out of doing so. Was he, too, treated in the same way in his young age and was venting it on them? Shiva secretly wondered.

The company, which built steam boilers, had been started by their employer—a person they used to call 'Baba'—a nickname for elderly people in many parts of India—who had been a worker with some experience and was brimming with confidence. He had started out entirely on his own and Shiva always admired his courage and zeal. However, what Shiva learned from him in life was not something he *wanted to do*, but things that he *should not do*.

There were four executives in the company, including Shiva—one for Accounts, one for Service, one for Production, with Shiva in sales. The rest of the employees were all daily-wage workers. With the kind of work and compensation that was dished out to them, Shiva's pride in calling themselves 'engineers' took a huge beating. Shiva used to go to office and sit there, calling up people to ask about their requirements and generate inquiries. In those days, there was only limited dial-in Internet and a Yellow Pages book to facilitate whatever it was that he was doing. Sometimes, Shiva used to wonder whether, in fact, he was a Sales Executive or a Telephone Operator.

Shiva was getting more and more dispirited calling people up on the phone using the Yellow Pages and would think, "This isn't what I wanted. I need to grow, find more about how actual sales deals are struck, and interact more directly and more often with potential customers and clients."

One morning, despite a busy work schedule, Shiva confronted Baba openly. "Baba, I'd like to go out to the field and talk to more people face to face," he blurted out.

Baba's lips convulsed in a grimace that was a mixture of scorn and wry amusement. "Don't you know that these are trying times and going out to the field would burn an enormous hole in my pocket? Use the telephone to generate inquiries. That's what the bloody instrument is there for!"

Shiva said no more. But that was the time when he firmed up his decision not to stay on any longer in the company.

"I won't be reporting for work from tomorrow," Shiva said, managing a weak—but determined—smile.

Baba was aghast...and at a loss for words. He had not expected this. At all!

Shiva still leant on this lesson he had learnt early in his career and never demeaned any of his subordinates, or fellow workers. Ever! **He always treated them the way he had wanted to be treated!**

Shiva knew instinctively then 'What *Not* to Do'... He decided that day not to carry on in that company for a single more day. He knew then that not only had he to walk away, but knew instinctively *he had to run...* And no, Shiva was not counting his money. Yet! There would be time enough for counting, later... 'DESTINY' had not quite finished dealing his cards!

Chapter III

How Choice Shapes Destiny

What You Must Do

'In life, you have three choices.
Give up,give in, or give it your all'

JOBLESS AND ADDING to the small 'family' of theirs cooped up in the sparsely furnished, somewhat rundown and dingy tenement room at the lower end of town was nothing short of hurting. But Shiva and his friends managed to keep their spirits high. The rest of his friends who were also part of this happy—sometimes not-so-happy—family sharing each moment of their lives were a thoroughly worried lot. How they would manage their expenses, which were not insignificant by any stretch of imagination, was the question that dominated most of Shiva's waking—even sleeping—hours.

But, somehow, they did not show it on their faces, speaking words of encouragement now and then, spurring Shiva on to find a job which would lead to fulfilling his dreams. *He* did the same for *them*. Once you are used to getting paid—even meagre amounts of daily wages—things are manageable. But when you do not have money and savings have been a pipedream, the tap is closed and it is time to look to your parents for help.

But Shiva knew that his parents already had their hands full of trouble. They had to take care of his younger brother and sister and spent huge amounts on providing for them, especially on their education. Paying for Shiva's Engineering course had already taken a huge toll on his meagre savings. So, for Shiva, that door was closed. One rainy afternoon that was overcast with clouds, feeling desperate and dejected, Shiva just called up his Dad to tell him that he had become jobless and how he felt. His father encouraged Shiva to look around a little more and find one.

Finding a job in those times despite his father's constant encouragement was considerably more expensive than in the present times. In those days, there was no Internet other than the cost-prohibitive dial-up, mobile phones, or job portals. The only way was to reach out to job consultants, or print hundreds of copies of your resumé and then move around the industrial area and drop them off to the security man at the gate. The telephone number on the resumé was, more often than not, the landline phone of your neighbour, so that, if by chance the employer needed to get in touch with you, they would reach out on that number.

But the calls never came! After making endless rounds of the offices in the industrial hub and endless days of waiting, one day, Shiva happened to visit a placement agency's office. It was his temple in those days. Just as we enter a temple to pray, Shiva used to pay regular visits there and prayed that they find him a job. That day, the placement assistant had an opening where he wanted Shiva to go along with a few more candidates.

"It's a sales job—right up your street," he smiled encouragingly.

Shiva was being interviewed by a middle-aged, bald man with a paunch, in a waistcoat two sizes too small for him. He still recalled the question which, he believed till this day, was the tipping point in securing the job for him.

"Where do you want to see yourself in the next 5 years?" he asked. It was one of the commonest questions doing the rounds at interviews in those days—and still does today.

But Shiva adroitly skirted the question, avoided a direct answer and, puffing up his chest slightly, said importantly, “I’d like to be a Marketing Director by age 30!”

The next question was “How?” So, Shiva told him how long he would stay there and how he would jump from one position to the next in hierarchical transition to reach his goal. He was impressed and hired Shiva straightaway. There, he learned a lot about sales and it was a game-changer in his learning curve. The basis of what *not* to do had already been created at Baba’s place. Now, Shiva needed to learn what *to* do and *how* to do it! The salary was not anything to write home about, but Shiva was not complaining. It was still a huge jump compared to the measly wages he had been getting in his last job!

***

In life, Shiva came across many people who curse God, or ‘destiny’, for the very misadventures that they, themselves, have brought upon them. However, he had hardly seen anyone taking responsibility for the choices they had made and then say in a Cartesian philosophical vein, “I am, because of the choices I made.”

Many choices are made through conscious decisions and some are made through unconscious ones. Those who can judge the difference between being conscious of the choices they make have succeeded in life and built a greater edifice of life from whatever the world has thrown at them; the rest are living at the 'mercy of someone else who wrote their destiny'.

But, honestly speaking, what *is* the difference between choice and destiny? If you believe that the world revolves round the conscious and subconscious choices that we make, you regard that your life is the product of the decisions that you have made. But, if you blindly believe in the power of destiny, you are simply placing the responsibility on higher forces that define your life's story.

Billy Graham had once famously said, "The strongest principle of life and blessings lies in our choices. Our life is the sum result of all the choices we make, both consciously and unconsciously."

***

SHIVA WAS STILL WORKING as an Assistant Product Manager when, one lethargic, hot afternoon in 2007 loaded with paperwork, he got a mass e-mail message from the US-based multinational that was looking for a Regional Manager for India to start their Indian operations.

With a total of barely seven years of sales experience, Shiva pushed himself to avail of this opportunity. He appeared for the interview and waited for quite a while. The final interview for the post took another six months. When you are young, you tend to be impatient and Shiva nearly gave up. Then, when the offer materialized six months later, he was even more surprised to see that they were willing to give him whatever he had asked for.

Shiva started out as Regional Manager to establish the company's business in India from scratch. The management had decided to build a manufacturing plant in India. With his industrial sales background, he accomplished difficult tasks, like renting an industrial facility, setting up a manufacturing unit and complying with numerous legal requirements.

Given Shiva's experience—or rather inexperience—of all this, it was a tall order for him! But when you have the will, you find the ways and means. The journey was not quite a cakewalk; it had its ups and downs. As a new business, even hiring the right people was a challenge as working with startups was not such a cool thing in those days. It was tough to sell products manufactured in India as, in this country, industrial equipment sells mostly on sound references. And Shiva and his team had none!

Hiring! Shiva didn't demur to say that he, personally, had made a great many mistakes in hiring people and the process is not as simple as the HR resource books would make it out to be. It had brought upon him not only a lot of embarrassments in his professional life, but also endless trouble.

Hiring a wrong candidate who does not fit into your requirement parameters and is judged by mere one or two rounds of interviews may cause a lot of heartburn later. Frankly, we tend to believe many statements that a candidate who is well-versed and groomed in interview techniques by modern B-schools makes. But these may be far from the truth and the reality is revealed only when he or she starts working on the ground.

The memory of one of Shiva's HR classes at a premier management institute in the country was still fresh in his mind. What the professor had said then became clear to him now. But it was a bit late as most of his employees had already been hired by him and working for the past 10 years or so. When we hire someone, we always expect them to do what we feel is right. But again, there is a shift of perception between the two.

It is said that good leaders can convince people to work along the lines delineated by the company to achieve certain goals and motivate them at all times. This may be true to a limited extent. But, when you hire a person and he loses his alignment, it makes for a tricky and difficult situation.

Someone may seem to—or, actually—have been good when you hired him eight years ago. And then, you keep 'developing', or moulding, that person according to your company's requirements. But, when the economies of scale hit your business, they may not be the right fit to handle the pressures of the deliverables and the deadlines. In such a scenario, training and motivation—all become important. But time runs out fast, too, and to catch up with the market pressures, you hamper your growth.

Now, the rule book says, 'You should be a visionary', and Shiva totally agreed. But visionary people also need to gauge their own limitations at their end and the limitations of their circumstances. At the same time as you want to grow, you cannot afford to hire someone on a higher salary at that level. So, you have to deal with people you have got and upskill them to take up higher responsibilities. If things get aligned and the workflow is smooth, things turn out all right. But, if not, then trouble starts mounting. Catching up with this backlog becomes difficult for the 'visionary' and, granted his aptitude of understanding people, he may go wrong, as well!

Honestly, Shiva was still grappling to fill this kind of a void and might continue to do so until he set things right. But no two people are alike. Everyone has to be trained, motivated differently. When you are a small company, as the India presence—or absence?—of the company when Shiva joined its country operations, things are fairly easy and the difficult parts of the jigsaw puzzle fall into place. But, as one grows, one feels disconnected as one's time is taken up by many other pressing matters. And there comes the real challenge of time management. How to stay connected with people at all times, even when away from office or plant?

Shiva once knew the Chairman of a large conglomerate. He had naïvely asked him, "How do you manage such a large organization?"

His prompt reply was simple, but very effective, "I have good people with me."

At that moment, Shiva remembered a story about Ramakrishna Paramhansa and Swami (Narendra) Vivekananda. He wasn't sure if anyone would agree with him, but it was Vivekananda who made Ramakrishna famous across the world. Vivekananda was a disciple of Ramakrishna, and the latter would have been relegated to the faded pages of East India's history if the former had not been there.

One needs disciples like Vivekananda who can take your name forward to make one proud. It is very important to find people who will take your visions further—which you may not be able to do all alone. Shiva still carried the Chairman's *mantra*: "*I have good people with me*" and was working on finding good people who could work towards the goal that he had established for his organization.

***

SHIVA MADE HIS FAIR SHARE OF MISTAKES, which, in the long run, taught him *which cards to throw away and which to keep*! The realization came with time and experience and, maybe, a few repetitions of mistakes, too. When he needed help or had to see things in a different perspective, he turned to self-help books to channel his thoughts in the right direction. His company's stakeholders lent a helping hand throughout.

A character in Paulo Coelho's famous book, '*The Alchemist*', says whoever you are, or whatever you do...when you really want something, it is because that desire originated in the "Soul of the Universe". It is your "Mission on Earth". When they first meet, Melchizedek speaks these lines to Santiago, which forms the basic tenet of the book.

To put all of this in perspective...we may strive continuously to achieve a goal and pin our hopes—vent our grievances—on the Almighty most of the time. That God helps only those who help themselves is a time-tested philosophy. But this is not the God who drops manna from heaven. It is your belief in Him that keeps your hopes alive and gives you the strength to pick yourself up every time you fall. And the circumstances turn in your favour rather than against you when you consciously, or unconsciously, keep working in the direction of your goals.

Test your experiences on the touchstone of failures and know where you are *not* supposed to venture, or which 'Lakshmanrekha' you *must not* cross. By cutting down on the 'no-go' areas, you keep increasing your chances of success by actually travelling in the right direction. People often say that you 'must keep going' whatever happens. You may fall, but those who get up again and resume their journey are successful.

But the simple reason why they succeed is because they have learnt from their experiences and understood what *does not* work, and, by a process of elimination, what *would* work instead. Reinventing yourself all the time is the essence of any success story. Keep reminding yourself which path you *should not* be taking, and so take the right turn at every turn. Every time!

If Shiva remembered correctly, it was, possibly, Charleston Parker, who in his book, '*One Soul, Many Faces—Revealing the Hidden Truth*', summed up the vital role that choices play in our lives. He said, "In life, you have three choices. Give up, give in, or *give it your all*!"

Chapter IV

Humility & the Big Picture

Early Lessons from a Mentor

A true leader is not only humble, but also has the ability to look at the entire canvas rather than focusing only on one aspect

EARLIER, IN 2002, the company Shiva had joined was run by a President who was an awe-inspiring personality, sufficiently advanced in his years to be at the helm of corporate affairs. The monthly review meeting had come up some time at the beginning of the third quarter of that financial year and, as the meeting was about to end, the President hooked his laptop to the projector. He had a screensaver showing him standing in the iridescent sunlight reflected off the deep snow at the foothills of a steep, snowcapped mountain range. Struck with awe, one of the executives in the conference room asked him where the photograph had been shot.

"Well, I've just been to the Himalayas and this photo was taken at the Dronagiri base camp. I just wanted to tell you all that, age notwithstanding, everything is possible if you have the desire to achieve your goal!" he said with an ill-concealed pride that showed on his face and in his body language.

Shiva was a young, aggressive sales executive in those days, and had been given the responsibility of Product Management which he considered a feather in his cap at that young age. So, with the full of enthusiasm and brashness of youth—Shiva was still not past 25 years at the time—he blurted out something stupid which he had not forgotten till this day.

"Sir, but I'm sure this picture has been Photoshopped!" A moment's silence fell on the room, only a brief one! Everyone froze into a hushed silence...

But the President of the company, who could even then have shown Shiva the door, said something he would always remember! With his usual, benign smile, he said, "Well, I've really been there; it's not just a Photoshopped picture. If you want, I can show you many more photos of me scaling the mountain to that height."

A suitably chastised Shiva believed the President and this seemingly insignificant episode was brushed under the carpet right there in the meeting-room as nothing but a joke. Later, however, his immediate boss did give Shiva a thorough tongue-lashing. "How on earth did you have the gall— the utter cheek—to say something like that to the President? It was sheer foolhardiness. Do you realize that you could have been thrown out of the company without notice for saying something like that?"

When we are young, we tend to make many mistakes and may get punished for our wrongdoings. But the moral of this short episode is that, even as the 'supreme commander' of the office, the President did not take umbrage at Shiva's temerity in making that rash comment, but showed him how humble he was and how nicely he could handle the situation without making Shiva feel inferior in front of all his seniors and peers. Shiva had learnt a big lesson that day! The President gave Shiva many motivational insights and ingrained into him many of the values—like humility, tolerance, and forbearance—that had contributed to making Shiva not only a better person to work with, but also developed crucial leadership qualities in him.

***

THERE WAS ANOTHER TIME, IN 2005, when the President sanctioned Shiva's trip to England and France to visit the company's principals for training. It was a kind of a bonus for him since he was then only three years old into the company and it was the older man's wise way of showing that Shiva was outperforming his peers. Well, Shiva had nothing to complain about...

For one week at a stretch in each of the countries, Shiva spent a splendid time. At a young age of 25-26, visiting the places was a much more pleasurable experience than the rigors of the training programmes. Getting one's passport stamped in foreign countries in those days was also gratifying. People gave one a lot of importance for a '*phoren* trip', which did wonders for one's ego.

Once Shiva's training in West Sussex, England, ended, the people who were responsible for that session and the overall programme took him to an Indoor Racing Competition. Shiva did not know how to drive a four-wheeler in those days and was only used to handling a motorcycle. But here, he got into a closed-circuit motor racing car which did not quite seem to obey his inept handling of the machine. No one was surprised that Shiva never finished a single lap and came in behind all the other contestants.

Well, there he was back in India and in his office discussing his trip to England and France with his immediate boss and the President. A great leader, the latter wanted to hear about all the business opportunities that Shiva had worked on. (Apart from undergoing training, he had also been given the vital task of meeting the heads of two new companies and discussing the potential of being their Indian partner for meeting their sales targets in the Indian market). Simply put, Shiva was the face of those companies in India. So, the President wanted to know particularly about these meetings and Shiva explained to him what exactly had transpired and how he had succeeded in fuelling their business interests.

At the end of an hour-long discussion over a cup of coffee and a plate of cookies, Shiva told him about the motor racing he had gone to. As he never knew how to drive a four-wheeler and had come in last behind three other contestants, Shiva simply mentioned that he had come in at fourth place in the race.

"How many contestants were there?" the President abruptly threw the question at Shiva without giving him time to think.

Caught off-guard, Shiva stammered out an admission. "There were only four, Sir..."

Shiva had learnt another lesson that day—the importance of observing the big picture rather than focusing on just one aspect. A true leader always looks at the entire canvas rather than concentrating only on one quadrant. A good leader has a broader perspective and a clearer vision than others as from high on a mountaintop. From atop the Dronagiri? mused Shiva.

***

THE PRESIDENT HAD CHOSEN SHIVA over quite a few aspirants who were also in the reckoning for a post to handle sales across entire India. (He was now handling this job for his current company for the past sixteen years). Meanwhile, Shiva was in a dilemma over joining a new company that had approached him with an enticing job offer. But that company was not heard of in those days. It was just a small, family-run business in the US—never mind how big the Tatas and the Birlas were in India—although a very old one. But it was a risk Shiva was willing to take given his young age.

Almost past 5.30 one evening—Shiva still remembered he was about to wrap up his work for the day and write out his daily report—when the President summoned him to his chamber to discuss his future in the company and how he wanted Shiva to take up new responsibilities as he was not only doing well, but had far surpassed the company's expectations. Shiva was in a pickle, to use a cliché—although clichés very well sum up certain situations and that is why they become clichés! What irony! There he was, waiting to resign from the company and, at the same time, discussing his future assignment with the seniormost employee of the organization.

Shiva asked himself a simple question: "Is it ethical to move on when your company depends so much on you?" And he got a silent answer in his head immediately. Yes, Shiva's ethics *did* allow him to move ahead. *He had to know what to throw away and what to keep!* Abruptly, as if some external force had made him blurt out, Shiva cried, "Sir, I may not be able to carry on according to your plan as I'm thinking of moving to a much bigger role in another company!"

There was a stunned silence. Shiva had expected a violent and indignant outburst. Maybe, also a few words of sentimental trash? He was still not sure how he would have handled the situation then if he had been in the President's position. But the way he reached out to Shiva was amazing and left a great impression on him.

"And what's this new company that's offering you the job, son?" he asked Shiva simply. "How did you get to know of them—or did they approach you first?"

Shiva believed then—as he still did now—in candid speaking. So, he asked the President if he would be a good fit for the company. "The company I'm about to join doesn't have any presence in India as of now. I've been tasked to build their India operations from scratch."

Shiva still credited him for his insight into his abilities and encouraging him wholeheartedly to take up the job as it was, indeed, a good opportunity.

"You may age—and age gracefully into a grey-haired boss—in this company if you don't take the risk and take up this offer. But then, when will you get a chance again...if ever? Remember, opportunity doesn't knock on the same door twice. All my blessings will always be with you, my son... go ahead." Did Shiva detect a faint tremor in the President's voice as he spoke in a low tone? He couldn't quite say!

The President's stunning response was—and will always be—a motivation for Shiva all his life. He was moved by this simple, unassuming speech. As time passed, he moved on, but met the President several times even afterwards to seek his advice—and blessings. Shiva realized how genuine and down-to-earth a person the President was and his guiding light and soft encouragement had propelled Shiva to the position he held right now. Helping one to take a decision and move on even when you know you are losing the services of an able and efficient person who was delivering the goods for your organization is a task of selfless service by one's superior—just let's say 'first among equals', shall we?

Chapter V

Patience, Persistence, PR

Sales Lesson over Idlis and Dosa

The more fortitude we show,
the better the gains in terms of prices
while negotiating commercially.

This is a game-changer
Shiva learnt that day

MANY YEARS LATER, SHIVA would speak to his juniors about one of the sales assignments that he and his colleague had been tasked to carry out in the past. People in sales who have difficult quotas to fulfil would, possibly, relate with the circumstances as their own. These unsung heroes of small and big companies in the frontlines of a never-ending battle—whose efforts against all odds are never acknowledged except with incremental salary hikes, or with a 'ribbon of success' at a year-end R&R get-together—are always under severe pressure to meet their targets.

Shiva and his friend were targeting one of the oil and gas projects awarded to a private company, which would not allow his company a foothold—not even a toehold!—and always kept fobbing them off with bland excuses saying they were too late. Despite this, his colleague from Chennai, KM Vani, and Shiva kept knocking on the door of their Bangalore office every single day of the week. They managed to find out who the person in charge of technically finalizing the deal was before they would approach the Commercial Manager.

They kept fruitlessly trying to fix up a meeting with him even as he kept avoiding them on one pretext or the other. To say that Shiva felt extremely frustrated would be an understatement. He remembered wondering what on earth they were doing, wasting their time, since that company did not have any intention of entertaining their sales pitch, at all. Their competition, Company X, had a former employee of their potential client as its Head of Sales. So, things were bad from the very beginning. They were fast losing all hopes of closing the deal and felt the job would be awarded to their competitor X.

Knowing one's offer is being stonewalled at the initial step of the process is the worst-case scenario for any sales person to face. They had already wasted enough time! When Shiva discussed this with his boss, she said, "Don't worry. Stay back in Bangalore as long as it takes for you to sign the deal. The company will bear all your expenses. You'll surely find a way past that man, however impregnable a fortress he may have built around him."

She kept encouraging Shiva and Vani to keep up their morale, so, they were stationed in Bangalore for almost a whole month—planting their foot in their office door, so to say. Their food, accommodation and transport were a drain on the company's finances. But they persisted in the hope of one day being able to break the ice.

One afternoon around lunchtime, Shiva and Vani were waiting as usual for the person in charge of technical approval—let us call him Venu for convenience's sake—to emerge from his chamber even for a brief moment. Whenever he *did* come out, he would usually ignore their stoic presence in the waiting lounge. His eyes would look vacantly past them—and beyond them—in almost the unique way that a Brit ignores, or looks through, a person whose presence he, or she, wishes not to acknowledge. And, if by chance their gaze *did* meet, he would give them that cold, icy stare that they were getting to know quite well by now!

But Shiva and Vani's tenacity in making their presence felt in the waiting lounge almost every day of the week must eventually have cut some ice. One terribly hungry afternoon, Shiva got what you might call a brainwave. This being an industrial area, one did not find many eateries close to the office precincts. So, Shiva thought, "Why not eat lunch in the company cafeteria, right next to the waiting lounge?" But Vani was not too sure about this, because the difficult next step was *how* to do that, since the cafeteria was open only to employees of the company and visitors needed coupons from employees to eat there.

Shiva walked uncertainly up to Venu's chamber, tentatively knocked on the door and opened it after he heard a brief "Yes?" which was half-query and half-consent for him to enter the room.

Shiva asked him, "Sir, we're very hungry. We'd be grateful for some lunch in your cafeteria. Could you please give us two coupons...one for my colleague and another for me? We're famished! We don't have any transport, either, to go out some place nearby and eat..." The words rushed out of

Shiva all in one breath as he waited for Venu to explode and braced himself for being thrown out of the door.

Venu looked at Shiva for a brief while. He leaned back slightly in his chair. Shiva thought he saw the glimmer of an amused smile behind his thin, clipped Clark Gable moustache. He pulled open a drawer of the massive teakwood table in front of him and took out a coupon booklet. "All right," he said—Shiva felt he was *actually* enjoying playing the host—as he tore out two coupons, taking all the time in the world to do so, and handed them to him.

Shiva's heart leapt with joy! His words had cut ice with him. Finally! They had just had a *two-way dialogue*, however brief! A ticket to more conversation... And, far above the Dronagiri range of mountains, the sun glimmered in a faint ray of hope. Shiva felt as if he had been in a long meeting with him with that short conversation.

It was a big moment for Shiva and Vani. Enough to savour—and celebrate with—the two plates of *idlis* and a *dosa* each that the cafeteria boy placed before them, for that is all that they could bring themselves to sponge on this man's kindness that day! The smoking plate of aromatic *Gobi Manchurian* that the boy carried across the room to the other table right in front of their noses could wait. Till another day!

***

FROM THAT MOMENT ONWARDS, the tide seemed to turn in their favour. The next day, to their surprise, while Shiva and Vani were stationed in the waiting lounge, Venu stepped briskly up to them. "I'm going for lunch," he said, "Would you both like to join me?" Things had changed dramatically and the wind seemed to be blowing strongly in their favour. They were actually talking business over a lunch of hot rice, *sambhar*, *rasam*, mixed vegetable curry, *Gobi Manchurian* (the signature dish of Bangalore), *happala* (Kannada for *papad*) and sour curd.

But Shiva do not for a moment believe that it was just the lunch coupons that had turned the tide in their favour. There was their unmistakable, unshakeable presence in the waiting lounge whenever Venu would pass by and ignore them. As inevitable as the hands of the clock that moved indefatigably towards lunchtime! Venu must have noticed them then—marvelled at their persistence?—and may have been *testing their patience* to see how far they could *test the waters*. The more fortitude one shows, the better the gains in terms of prices while negotiating commercially. This is a game-changer that Shiva learnt that day. It was a huge project and involved an order value worth crores of rupees.

That is not the end of this interesting story. As Shiva and Vani were earning brownie points in their race to secure the order—they were also secure in their knowledge that they were technically better than their competitors—they had a sudden setback! The entire team of their competitors—the ex-employee, along with a few foreigners full of highfalutin marketing balderdash, no doubt—turned up in the waiting lounge a couple of days later. Shiva and his friend knew most of them, but the newcomers did not know *them*. As the Head of Sales was an ex-employee and a close friend of the General Manager, they had come to interact with their world of seniors and peers in the company.

All of them walked straight into the General Manager's chamber. Here, Shiva thought the team made its first mistake as they seemed to ignore Venu totally. Meanwhile, both Shiva and his colleague got very worried thinking that the order would now be closed at the level of the General Manager, since the new team was discussing business with him as two friends and Shiva and Vani were discussing it with Venu, who was only second-in-command to the General Manager, who headed the company, although on extension.

While all this was happening in the General Manager's room, Shiva trooped down to the cafeteria with Vani in tow to have some tea and discuss what they should do in a scenario where their competitor seemed to have an edge over them—not technically, but mostly at a personal level. They spotted Venu at the far end of the cafeteria having tea all alone.

Realizing an opportunity, Shiva walked up to him and said, "Sir! I see that our competitors are discussing the project with the General Manager and I think we're set to lose the order. You've been very helpful to us and you also know that we're technically much superior to the competition. You asked me for the target prices this morning and I'll have to write to our Principal in the US who will be responding by this evening. I can offer you the prices, if that's alright with you. Do you think we still have a chance, or have things gone out of hand as it'll be purely the decision of your General Manager?"

Shiva had earlier tried to arrange his Senior's and Principal's meeting with the General Manager, but he knew that Venu had the last word on which vendor to choose, what prices to accept and what technical parameters to accept. Venu listened to Shiva with an impassive face that betrayed no emotion. He did not comment. He finished his tea and started to leave. Shiva was woebegone that their last rescue rope had gone and all the positive hype they had developed with Venu might well go down the drain as his boss still held the power to take the final call.

Venu stood up and said with an expressionless face, "Remember, no order will get processed unless I say 'yes'." Shiva thought he heard, "I still *hold the ace*!" Somewhere, in his decisiveness, Shiva could hear the voice of *The Gambler*.

This was, undoubtedly, a big relief for Shiva and his friend because they knew how important bagging this project and beating the competition strategically was for their US Principal. That evening, Shiva got an okay from his Principal and they got the target prices indicated by Venu.

Thrilled with this new development, they rushed straight to Venu's chamber and almost shouted, "We have the prices you asked for and we can close the order right now, if you want."

It was close to 8.30 in the evening when they got the Letter of Intent before the Purchase Order went into writing. The competitor was also aware of what was happening since, being a former employee, he had his own contacts within this office. But there was precious little he could do about it, although he did try every dirty trick outside the rule book to slander them. Almost three months of stationing themselves in Bangalore—and returning home to Pune only on weekends—had finally paid off!

This story brings out a hugely important point: Find the 'right person'—as many sales training books state—decision-maker, influencer and user. In Venu, they had found all three combined and he was their 'influencer' with the General Manager. Their Patience, Persistence and PR with Venu—always being there to answer his queries and fulfil his order specifications—gave them that winning edge.

Almost six months after securing this order, Shiva left the company and moved on in life to take up greater responsibilities. He donned the mantle of India-Head of his present US-based company which wanted to start their business in this country and planned to set up a manufacturing facility here.

Chapter VI

Watchword: Value Selling

Confident, *Not* Presumptuous!

'If you're gonna play the game boy,
you gotta learn to play it right'

– Don Schlitz in 'The Gambler'

AFTER MOVING INTO HIS NEW ROLE, Shiva had many challenges ahead of him. He had always been in sales and marketing from the beginning of his career. But now, the challenge was production. The funny thing was that, although he had done his graduation in Production Engineering, he had no clue to how production happens in factories in real life. He believed studying in a college and working in the industry vastly differed in reality. Industry teaches you things you can never learn in a college classroom and that is where experience counts.

Shiva and his small group of helpers started out by testing the waters in India. A 168-year-old business in the US run by one family for four generations, the company had decided to come to the Indian shores to set up shop. They had already set up base in China in the 1990s and were doing moderately well there. Now, it was India they were targeting to mark their footprints in the country.

Being the oldest brand in the field, almost everyone in the US knew about the company and its products. The company was well known in the process industry, mainly among MNCs that had come from the US. So, they started exploring the markets of those US companies that had wide-scale operations in India. It took them a good amount of time to start their production unit in full swing and, in 10 years, they had reached a multi-crore-rupee business in India, besides supporting their US facility with a wide range of products.

But it was not at all easy to start with! They met various potential customers and everyone had a few very simple questions to ask, "Where have you sold your products?" or, "Who's your competition?" or, "Have you supplied to any industry like ours?"

Focusing more on the questions to provide inputs should help sales people tackle these kinds of situation.

"Where have you sold your products?" or, "Who's your competition?" have almost the same meaning. Being a 100% US-owned company in India, they had policies which they had to strictly adhere to. They had been told never to disclose who their customers were. In those early years, Shiva often struggled to understand what the problem with *that* was—why couldn't they reveal their customer database, or provide information on which customers they had supplied to? But no! The management stuck firmly to its point of view and warned them to refrain from disclosing their customer database to those they were targeting.

Sensing Shiva's growing frustration, his boss called him one day to tell him exactly why they were doing so. Since the business was 175 years old by then, it had supplied its products to multiple customers over the past many decades and had signed non-disclosure agreements, or NDAs, with them. They could not quite keep track of what had been written in those past NDAs. And, since the US is a country where one can file a legal case even if one's food is not served properly—and win, as well—their predicament was understandable.

All this was simple enough for Shiva to understand. But to convey that understanding to his sales team was the first difficult task before him. And it did not end there! Making each customer back in India understand the same thing was extremely tough given the culture we are born and brought up in. But Shiva had to abide by the rules his US bosses had laid down for him.

This had a hugely negative impact on their operating style initially, since the chances were high that a customer would not look at buying their products without even knowing who their past clients were. Human emotions also played a significant part in this. Their first feeling was, “Oh! I asked you for certain information, but you refused it to my face! Not acceptable, at all.”

Often, this emotion would take the form of, “What harm could there be in revealing your customer database? I’d asked for it as I’d then be able to better gauge your brand value in the market. The bigger the conglomerates that have bought from you are, the better you are as a company. Simply sustaining for 175 years through all the turmoil of the world economy and going through the ravages of two World Wars doesn’t necessarily buy credibility for your brand.” Incredible! But this is what it is in real life.

Shiva still felt a sense of pride in being associated with such an old brand that never once diverted from its basic line of business, while many startups—he preferred to call them upstarts!—that have reached a multi-billion-dollar turnover have had to migrate from their primary line of business and diversify into something very, very different from where they started.

In sales, once you have provided the information sought, you will face a second question; and, once the second is answered, you will have a third with many more to follow.

We deal with customers in our day-to-day life. That is nothing new. A company is made up of people handling various departments. But, if you look deep into the mind of your customer, he has to be first satisfied that this brand is being used by others. Now, they will spring another question: "Have you supplied for such kind of and industry?" If your answer is, "Yes," the next question will be, "For what kind of applications?" If your answer is still in the affirmative, he may say, "Well, take us there." In other words, "Show us your worth?" As a buyer, he wants to save his skin from making a wrong purchase!

But, when you say that you cannot—as you have a 'No' somewhere down the line as it is against business ethics to take a potential customer who could be a competitor to your existing customer—you stand to ruffle many feathers! Shiva had seen many sales and marketing personnel take along their potential customer, or their employees, to visit their existing customer's plant. He was quite old-fashioned in that he believed it was not good ethics for any business to stoop so low and get their image tarnished. Just imagine if it had happened to your own company! The sales person is, after all, the brand ambassador of your company!

So, Shiva would always throw the question back to the customer whom he was trying to impress, "Will you be fine with it if I got your competition into your plant once I've supplied you the goods?"

But no... that was not acceptable, at all! "How could you ever think of such a thing?" Shiva could almost hear the exasperation in their voices. The powers that be who were ever ready to visit their competition—or at least scam their database out of Shiva—would never allow *their* competition to visit *their* plant.

This is one lesson for many in our country's sales brigade who think that, just by throwing references at potential clients—call it 'name dropping' if you wish to—they can garner more business. If this principle had been true, Shiva's parent company would have shut shop long, long ago. *Value selling is much more important rather than selling products.* When we talk of strict ethics and *no wrongdoings*, we create better value than leaving our dealings wide open for someone to inspect and betraying the *trust* your present client has in you. Encourage *value selling*, rather than *product selling*.

***

THERE IS AN OFT-QUOTED marketing dictum: "*Price can never exceed the value of a product.*" What values your product can bring to the user or the buyer need to be emphasised. That would be a better way to negotiate a sale. Shiva remembered one meeting with their potential customer to strike a deal worth around a million dollars right there on the table for them to pick up!

It had the same kind of start to the negotiations: "Which customers have you supplied your products to? Give us a reference list for similar capacities supplied to similar industries."

Having worked in the industry for 10 years earlier to this meeting, Shiva had been dealing with such kinds of questions till his hair had grown more than slightly grey! He thought, “Let’s make a deal with the customer and see how he reacts!”

Shiva spoke out aloud, “All right, I’ll provide you the reference—but what will you gain out of it, really? Will you remove the warranty clause from the order? Will you find it acceptable if, after your visits for reference, the equipment performance at your site is not within our scope to recalibrate?”

The client was a wizened old guy who understood perfectly in which direction Shiva was headed. He, too, had grey hair and the wrinkles of his skin spoke out clearly that he was much more worldly wise than Shiva was. Such questions created in his client a certain confidence in Shiva and his products, and his team was able to close the deal. They had a million dollars on the table to show for Shiva’s newfound wisdom. Nothing was done apart from a few words transacted from his lips to his potential client’s ears. The ability to make someone understand really depends on how confident you are about your product and services and it says everything about you and your company! *And, finally, Shiva was counting his money* only after *the dealing was done*! *And* The Gambler *would have wanted another swallow from Shiva’s nearly drained bottle before he faded off into an ever-lasting sleep.*

They say, when you have confidence, you can break all barriers *provided you play the game which does not hurt the customer's ego*. Human beings are egotistic and need others to handle their emotions when they grow in age and experience. Many would say, "That's not quite right!" and they, too, could have their own perspective. But Shiva's experiences told him otherwise.

Chapter VII

Negate Negativity

Let *No* One Tell You That You *Can't*!

Focus on what you want to be and things will fallin place; Do the right things and the right things will happen to you

ALTHOUGH SHIVA WAS NOT anywhere close to being a celebrity—nor did he have aspirations of becoming one—he was what one might call 'satisfied'. He was not, indeed, someone who had achieved the farthest milestone in his life, but whatever he *had* achieved was worth it if one considered the background he came from. So, he took pride in all his achievements and was always grateful for the redemptive circumstances he found himself in and for the Almighty's constant blessings showered on him all the time.

And his not-so-mean achievements had one driving force—F-O-C-U-S! Simply put, to persevere with his thoughts despite having a lot of people around him who would tell him a hundred reasons and excuses why they thought he could not do it.

Shiva remembered a story he had heard when he was very young.

Two close friends in their early teens were on their way back to their village after visiting a local circus that had pitched camp next to the nearby woods. One of the youngsters was lean, weighing around 20 kg, and the other a bulky adolescent, weighing around 42 kg.

On their way back, the bulky friend wanted a drink of water, so they stopped near a well. But he slipped and fell headlong into the well. Now, it was impossible for the thin friend to pull someone twice his weight out of the well. Nevertheless, he decided to try his best and threw down a rope—it was tied to a bucket meant to draw water out of the well—to his friend. And heave-ho! He got his friend out after immense effort. His love for his friend was so strong that he did not realize how he had managed to get someone double his weight out of that deep well.

Once back in their village the bulky friend narrated their story to the village folk. The news spread like wildfire and both friends kept talking about it to anyone who cared to listen. But no one was willing to believe, thinking they were spinning a yarn. So, the villagers decided to approach an old, wise man who would be able to solve this riddle.

The wise old man listened carefully to both the friends narrate their story—how the bulky one had clung on for dear life to the lifeline his friend had thrown in for him, how the scrawny one had tied his end of the rope to a big boulder lying near the wall of the well and how there was a time when he had almost given up but desperation lent him the strength and courage to achieve a near-impossible feat.

The wise man turned towards the crowd of people waiting for his pronouncement. The villagers, one and all, thought that he, too, would reject the children's story as far-fetched and preposterous. But the old man nodded affirmatively and said, "If the kids are saying this, it *must* be true." A collective gasp of exasperation came from the crowd. "How could this be true?" The wise man said simply, "Because there was no one there to tell the child, 'You can't'."

***

THIS STORY HAD MADE such an impression on Shiva that every time he was pushed to the edge with everyone saying 'No', he would leave no stone unturned in his search for ways to get it done. He felt thankful that he had been successful on most occasions.

Shiva knew that by focusing on what he wanted to do—what he wanted to be—would make things fall in place. He always believed in the dictum, "Do the right things and the right things will happen to you." The Internet was just taking baby steps in those days. Shiva's tectonic shift towards books as his sole companion—and not the kind he had studied in his college course—happened when he first read '*The Power of Positive Thinking*' by Norman Vincent Peale. He changed the way Shiva looked at the world.

Focusing on what one wants to be and sticking to one's field of work is the watchword. People gain experience only from repetitive jobs, or else one becomes 'master of none'. Repetitive jobs help a person gain mastery of that one path in life one chooses, although it may tend to become monotonous. But that is how we are wired. Even to be a good sportsperson, one must keep practicing the same sport for a major part of one's lifetime.

We have read many a time that Usain Bolt ran 100 metres in 9.58 seconds, then a world record.

But how many of us remember the time he spent to clock those 9.58 seconds? So, deciding what you want to achieve as early as possible, focusing on the end result, connecting it to your own passion or traits, and then breaking it down into smaller goals to reach bigger ones is a sure road to success.

***

THE WORD 'CAN'T' had made no sense to Shiva ever since he passed his Class XII Board examinations and decided against his father's wishes to relinquish the Tata Motors apprenticeship offer and continue studying a graduation course in engineering. In college, he had met Arvind, a thin, chain-smoking bespectacled young man with unkempt beard and an inevitable satchel slung from his shoulder. Arvind was two years his senior, but they were worlds apart in wisdom. Shiva used to look up to him for every small problem that cropped up.

One rain-swept afternoon, sitting in Arvind's 8'x8', dingy hostel room, Shiva had learnt, probably, what was the biggest lesson of his life.

"You know, Shiva... You can have anything, *any*thing at all in life that you wish to if you know just one thing. I'll let you in on my secret if you spare me a cigarette. I've just finished my packet,"

Arvind said, carelessly tossing out the butt end he was holding between his fingers through one of the two grilled windows of the room. *'And then, he bummed a cigarette,/ And then he bummed a light...?'* thought Shiva smiling to himself. Well, he was willing to part with a cigarette if this Gambler could give him some advice that he could keep!

Beyond the window was a narrow alleyway meant for use by sweepers with metal gates at both ends which used to be perpetually locked for reasons best known to the hostel caretaker. Nothing but an occasional errant cat ever strayed into the alley.

So, Arvind was on safe grounds using it as his extended ashtray as several clay pots in which he used to be served tea from the *chai* stall on the lane outside, which used to serve as his makeshift ashtrays, were filled to the brim, and overflowing. The butt end passed neatly through the grills on the window and landed on a garbage heap outside.

On the rough-edged wooden table that served Arvind as his study and dinner table combined was a huge pile of empty cigarette packets and matchboxes. Arvind picked up one, offered it to Shiva. "Throw it out of the window, quick!" he said.

Shiva did not know why he had to do it, or what purpose it would serve. He simply knew he had to, because Arvind had asked him to do it. He hardly, if ever, questioned Arvind...

Shiva picked up the cigarette packet and, with one clean sweep of his arm, flung the packet right out of the window.

"Good, now take this matchbox and throw it out," ordered Arvind. "Mind you, it has to go through at one shot."

Shiva picked up the matchbox, took careful aim and threw it with all the dexterity he could muster. The matchbox hit one of the grills, bounced back and lay still on the floor of the room.

"Never mind, try again...with another one," Arvind was firm, almost commanding, in his tone.

Shiva picked up another matchbox, aimed more carefully than before and threw it vigorously at the window. This matchbox, too, hit a grill and rolled back.

"Do it again, this time fast...!"

Shiva picked up another matchbox and, in the wink of an eye, threw it towards the window. And this time, it passed clean through! He looked at Arvind, questions on his mind.

"See Shiva, the first time you threw the cigarette packet out—it was much larger than a matchbox—you didn't even think twice. Your subconscious mind *knows* all the answers, including how to coordinate your mind, body and eyes. So, it passed through.

"But the next two times, even with much smaller matchboxes which ought to have cleared the grills with ease, you failed. That's because your conscious mind was busy grappling with the difficulties of the situation. What your conscious mind was actually doing was calculating the distance between the grills—which were your *doubts*—measuring the *impediments*, the *hindrances*, the *obstructions* to your plan which your subconscious mind would have overcome easily if you had kept *faith*! You did it with the *third matchbox*...

"Remember *at all times* to *keep faith* in your subconscious mind. That's why we have the saying in the *Gita*, "Belief helps you achieve material things (read Krishna, the embodiment of all your desires), debate pushes it farther away," or, as in the *Bible*, "Ask and ye shall receive." *That* asking has to be *total surrender* to the Almighty. Your subconscious mind is the Gateway to the Almighty. Trust it at all times…"

Chapter VIII

The King & the Beggar

Writing Your Own Obituary!

'You alone are real.
The 'you' who was present as pure consciousness in your dream state playing the role of beggar and the one who is present in your wakefulness playing the role of king...this YOU is your true reality'

SHIVA HAD A GREAT LOVE FOR BOOKS. His constant readings made him wiser and wiser as he continued with this habit. But, for everything, there is a takeaway. He read anything that even vaguely interested him irrespective of its usability in his current life. Slowly, that made him read more on spirituality and Vedic teachings, as well. And this moved him away more and more from earthy practicalities towards an inner search for the meaning of life as he continued reading weighty tomes by numerous spiritual leaders, past and present.

He came across a story of ancient India where Raja Janak had a dream during his after-lunch siesta. The King saw he had lost a battle and had to run for his life into the forest. He was extremely hungry and as poor as a pauper, looking for food. To satisfy the pangs of his hunger and thirst, he desperately approached a *langar* (a free community kitchen) in a village close by where food was distributed to the poor and needy.

But, even before he could reach there, the entire food was over and only a few grains of rice were left in the big, earthen pot. The person doling out the food felt pity on him and scraped the bottom of the vessel to gather together a handful of morsel for him to eat.

The King was handed the crumbs on a plate made from banana leaf and, just as he was about to have his first bite, a bird swooped down and the entire food fell from the plate to the muddy ground below. Much perturbed, the kind cried out in anguish and this cry woke him from his slumber. He was in his quiet, peaceful, serene palace, with a full stomach and his servants fanning him with handheld palm fronds and woven squares of bamboo strips hanging overhead. He wondered in surprise, "What *is* real? Is it I, the beggar, as in the nightmare or is it I, the King?"

His question was answered by the great sage, Ashtravakra. He said Rajan was neither the beggar in reality, nor a King. "You, alone, are real. The 'you' who was present as pure consciousness in your dream playing a beggar's role and the 'you' who is present in your wakefulness playing a King's role... this 'you' who witnessed both these states is your true identity.

"Life in the daytime is but an illusion...a daydream and, life in your sleep, a night dream, or a nightmare. They are both illusions, filled with defects and flaws because they constantly change from one to another; so, they cannot be real. Only 'you' will remain unchanged in all these states and that is real, free from all illusions," said Ashtravakra.

Shiva read many other stories and scriptures, but this was the story that moved him more than any other. He started looking at things differently—his perspective of life had changed. What is the purpose of everything we do and why, if reality is pure consciousness. Why does all humanity not just sit down and meditate on their consciousness rather than running around for unwanted, unwarranted materialism? Money is, indeed, necessary for life to carry on with the basic necessities. But how much is the question!

And so began Shiva's quest for self-realization, finding the meaning of life...

***

SHIVA, IN HIS QUEST to find the meaning and real purpose of life, slowly slipped into a depression. Nothing excited him, nothing made him happy, nothing saddened him...as if he had turned to stone, though stones don't feel hunger, don't feel hot or cold, don't feel sleepy! He did, all of these...

He read Swami Vivekananda, Ramakrishna Paramhansa, J Krishnamurthi, Osho and Sadguru and left almost none untouched, but, somewhere, he found they all spoke of the same things. His work was also aligned with his entire existence as he had never believed that work and life were different. But, somewhere, his changing perspective of life hit his work. And, somewhere, he was losing touch with what he had built up, so far.

Customer complaints, quality issues, employee attrition—almost everything which should not have happened—started snowballing all at once.

He could not understand why things were not going quite the way they should even as his mind grappled with the complexities of life more than with the loads of work piled up on his office table. He was not able to comprehend the turmoil of this phase of his life. And things were slowly, but surely, slipping away from his hand as water flowing from a leaking tank.

An echo of Melchizedek's lines to Santiago in Paulo Coelho's '*The Alchemist*', "Whoever you are, or whatever you do...that desire originated in the 'Soul of the Universe'. It is your "Mission on Earth", still reverberated in Shiva's mind.

And, maybe in consonance with that 'mission', he happened to be approached by a premier institute for a four-day programme on '*Transformational Leadership—Finding your Purpose in Life*', conducted by Professor Ram.

The programme started at an odd time, 5 o'clock in the evening, which slightly surprised Shiva. When he reached the venue, there were 20-odd senior leaders in their respective fields who also looked surprised and confused. Some joked, "Are we having a party tonight? At what time do we start?" They all entered the classroom meant to accommodate a batch of only 25, sitting in a semi-circle in plush chairs which gave the feeling that this class would be something worthwhile.

Shiva was happy to see people of his age—or even older—and believed that they, too, had the same questions which were bothering him for years now. Professor Ram abruptly asked everyone to write their obituary and come for the class at sharp 9 am the next day. This took everyone by surprise! What *should* they write about in their own obituaries? Their life, hopefully, were not over yet! They did not understand until the next day...

Shiva flopped onto his bed, tired from the long, early morning flight, meeting a few clients in the region and then attending the evening session. After he had freshened up a little, he sat down to write his own obituary. But he soon found out that he could write only on aspects related to his entity as a living being with nothing to write on that was even vaguely morbid in nature.

No, not even anything that related to his materialistic self. Not a single statement spoke about all that he had done in his life, about the materialistic acquisitions he had made, the heights of success he had scaled. He found he could only write on how nice a person he was, how caring a husband and dutiful a father he was, how helpful to the next man he was. After he had finished writing, he sat down and contemplated on the piece of paper in front of him that bore his imprint on it as a human being. And only then did he understand why Professor Ram had assigned him this task!

The programme went well the next day and lots of questions which had been bothering Shiva were answered. Somewhere, he felt he needed someone who could help him navigate his life further. His long-time acquaintance, Puspendra, whom he met at one of the symposiums he attended became his close friend. One day, Pushpendra approached him, saying that he was doing a course to become a coach to people to help them achieve higher goals and would continue working after his retirement which was due in a year or so. During his training as a coach, he needed volunteers whom he could coach experimentally as stipulated by the course.

He asked Shiva if he would like to be a part of it and Shiva was more than happy to agree to the proposal. This was a turning point for Shiva. He had now found someone who could hold the mirror to him and tell him whether what he was doing was what he wanted as there were several aspects of his work life which were falling apart and which he needed to take care of immediately.

Shiva came to know later that some people refer to their life's unanswered queries as a 'mid-life crisis'. Pushpendra's coaching did a wonderful job for Shiva and he could collect all his mental and physical faculties to align with the current requirements of the business he was handling. Every minute detail was worked on and slowly brought back to their right perspective ensuring growth for his organization. One of Pushpendra's teachings that Shiva imbibed was that, if you want others to grow, you yourself have to grow, as well.

The 15th and last law, from John Maxwell's '*The 15 Invaluable Laws of Growth*', known as '*The Law of Contribution*', postulates that you cannot pass on to others what you yourself have not gone through. In other words, '*If you want to keep giving, you have to keep growing*'.

Even as the pandemic hit the populace at large in 2020, tearing lives asunder, it had little, or no, effect on Shiva as he had now grown more robust and resilient to pain and human foibles.

He started connecting with people more often, meeting friends oftener than he had done before, and taking time off for his family, moving on to a happier, more fulfilling life!

Chapter IX

Team Trip to the Top

An Inclusive Exercise To Create Ownership

The year Shiva took that trek, they all as a team got so immensely connected that everyone started looking at the common goals of the company, not only individual ones

IF SHIVA HAD IGNORED THAT MASS E-MAIL MESSAGE that reached his desk many, many years ago, he would not have been where he was today. All the circumstances that led up to it were part of Shiva's experiences that connected the dots to make his dream come true. And, today, Shiva was Managing Director of the same company—now grown to 150+ employees—whose foundation in India he laid almost 15 years back. Shiva felt glad that he could knit a wonderful family. Whether it concerned stakeholders, or customers, or suppliers...he would keep striving to add joy to the lives of people around him. His journey with the company continues till date.

Had his seniors, his team, his subordinates and his mentor not given Shiva the opportunity to fix his errors, he could not have reached where he was today....the pinnacle of self-made success! It was an amazing journey. Shiva had grown from a Regional Manager to Operations Manager to Director-India Operations just 24 days before he turned 30. He had, initially, planned to become Marketing Director, but now found himself wearing an even bigger hat!

Even though Shiva had spent his lifetime in medium-scale businesses, he vividly remembered one instance when they wanted to see growth in the organization. But the big question was how do they demonstrate to all their colleagues and staff that they *could* do what it takes to achieve it. They had all sorts of people—some thin, some fat, some fit, some squat... But the question was, "How do we connect them to a common goal?" Many companies hire experts for team-building exercises, but Shiva believed in doing it by themselves with no external trainers.

Shiva and his team had a daylong conference followed by a party in the evening which lasted till around 12 midnight, when they suddenly decided,

"Let's climb the fort which is near our conference venue." The 'fort' in question was Singhgad—originally known as Kondhana—in the Bhuleshwar ranges of Shyadari located 49 kilometres south-west of Pune city. The fort stood 1,312 metres above sea level overlooking a beautiful, rugged countryside.

The Battle of Sinhagad—also the Battle of Kondhana—had taken place when the forces of the Maratha Empire mounted an attack on the fort of Sinhagad during the night of February 4,1670. The Marathas later captured the fort.

Everyone at the party was curious to explore what the fort looked like. But some felt inhibitions as it would, possibly, drain them of all their energy to be attentive enough at the conference the next day. Many were so drunk that they did not hesitate for a second to say, "Yes, *do* let us!"

Shiva said, "It's a commitment, so I'll wake you guys at 5 o'clock in the morning," although he, too, was quite inebriated. Still, he managed to wake up at 4.45 and awakened everyone in the other rooms of the hill base resort that they were stationed at for their sales and target-setting meet for the year ahead.

All of them joined in the quest to 'conquer' the hill-top—with the trek starting off from Singhagad Paytha in Donaje village—and climbed what had seemed an insurmountable mountain. It took them around 1 hour and 30 minutes of upward trek and 1 hour on the return. Then, they hit the conference room as scheduled. Everyone was excited. Many of them could not have imagined in the drunken stupor the previous night that they could ever do that trek after a late, late-night party and waking early to keep their word.

This activity was a team-building exercise, which is common with many organizations. On their part, the year that they made that trek they all, as a team, got so closely connected that everyone started looking at the common goals of the company and not only individual ones. This was the best way Shiva could ever have imagined communication to happen within the team. They were all engrossed in a win-win situation for everyone. Those who had stayed behind because of physical hindrances were supported by all and sundry to hit the top, not leaving a single soul behind!

www.ingramcontent.com/pod-product-compliance
Lightning Source LLC
LaVergne TN
LVHW041117150826
845673LV00007B/2097